# WONDERFUL WORDS

## On the
# GO!

First published in 2020 by Miles Kelly Publishing Ltd
Harding's Barn, Bardfield End Green, Thaxted, Essex, CM6 3PX, UK

Copyright © Miles Kelly Publishing Ltd 2020

This edition printed 2021

2 4 6 8 10 9 7 5 3

**Publishing Director** Belinda Gallagher
**Creative Director** Jo Cowan
**Senior Editor** Sarah Carpenter
**Designer** Venita Kidwai
**Production** Jenny Brunwin
**Image Manager** Liberty Newton
**Reprographics** Stephan Davis
**Assets** Lorraine King

ISBN 978-1-78989-115-7

Printed in China

British Library Cataloguing-in-Publication Data
A catalogue record for this book is available from the British Library

Made with paper from a sustainable forest

www.mileskelly.net

# WONDERFUL WORDS

# On the GO!

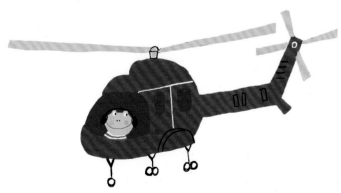

Illustrated by Ailie Busby

MILES KELLY

# On the road

There are lots of ways to travel by road – cars and buses can be different shapes and sizes.

people carrier

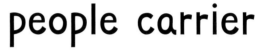

taxi

Can you find the pink pig?

limousine

saloon car

classic car

city car

sports car

jeep

Some double decker buses let passengers hop on and off so they can see the city sights.

Can you find the orange fox?

ROUTE 3

ALL ABOARD

rear platform

6

top deck

bendy bus

coach

driver's cab

How many cameras can you spot?

double decker bus

7

# To the rescue

If someone is hurt or in danger, these vehicles are sent to help!

siren

**police car**

POLICE

**ambulance**

**police motorbike**

POLICE

**police van**

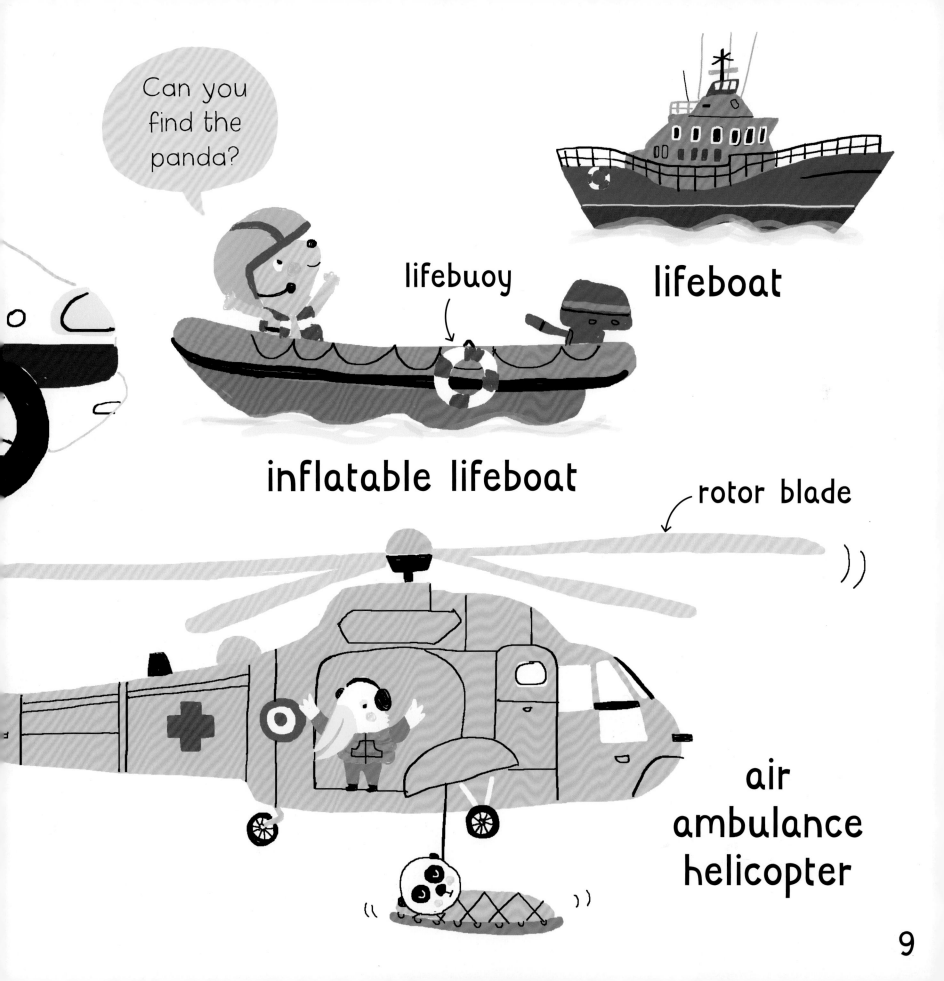

9

Firefighters drive special trucks to the scene of a fire.

**fire engine**

siren

firefighter

Can you find the number five?

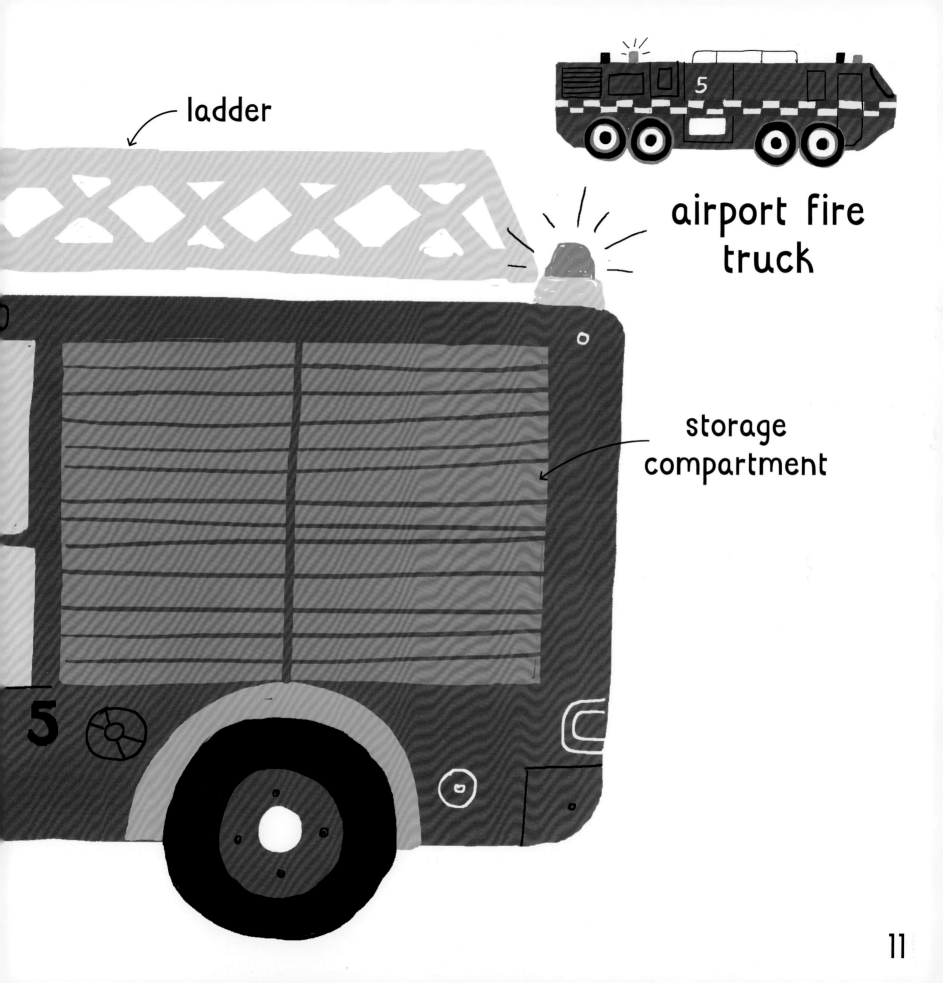

ladder

airport fire
truck

storage
compartment

5

11

# Wheelie wonders

Many bikes have two wheels, but some have three, or even just one!

What colour is my scarf?

unicycle

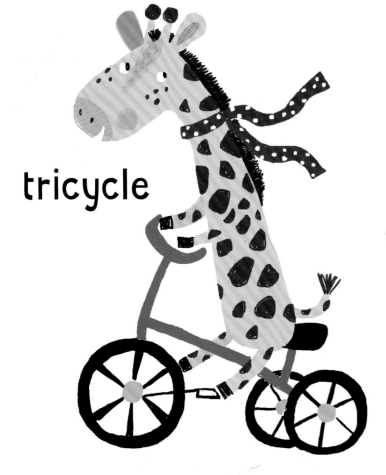

tricycle

tandem bike

Who is eating a lollipop?

handlebars

saddle

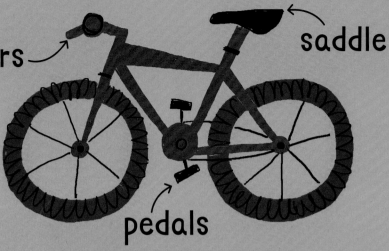

pedals

mountain bike

motorbike

scooter

lie-back tricycle

# Up, up and away!

Not all vehicles travel on the road – some move through the sky!

envelope

hot air balloon

What colours can you see on the hot air balloon?

gondola

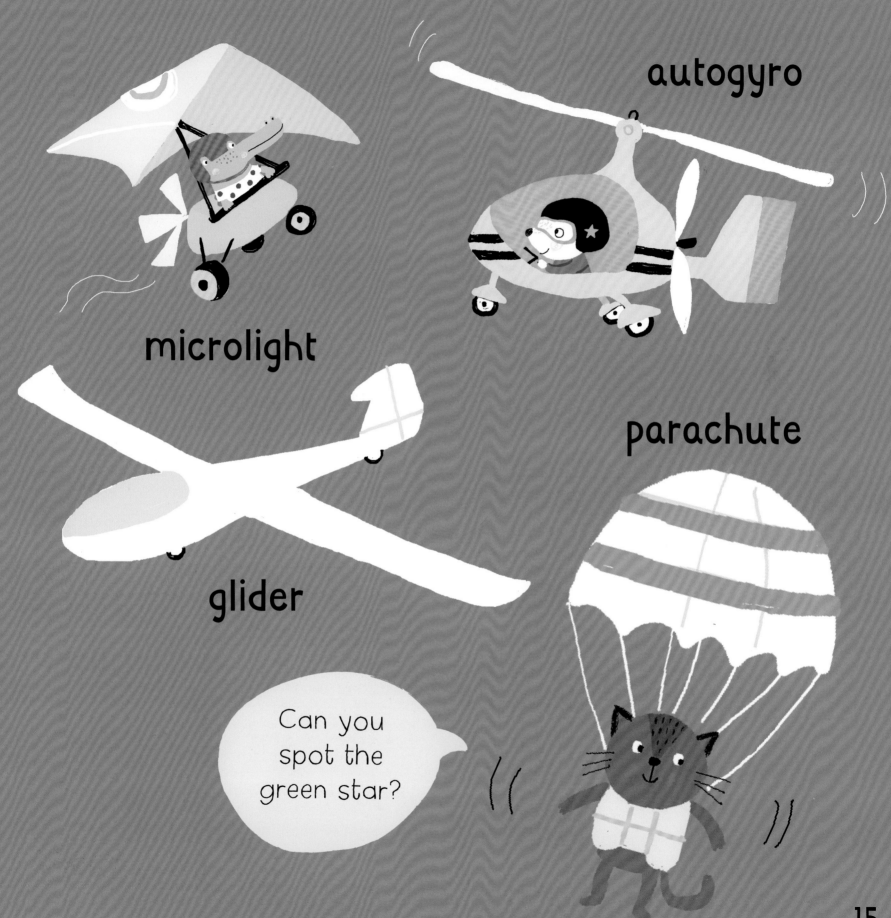

Some aircraft have wings and propellers to help them take to the sky.

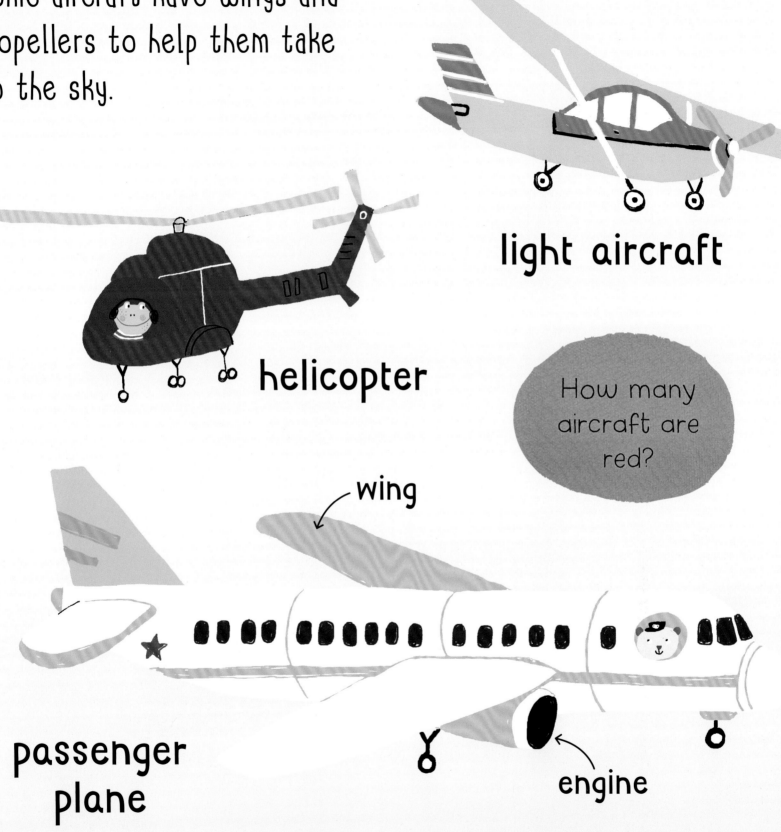

light aircraft

helicopter

How many aircraft are red?

wing

passenger plane

engine

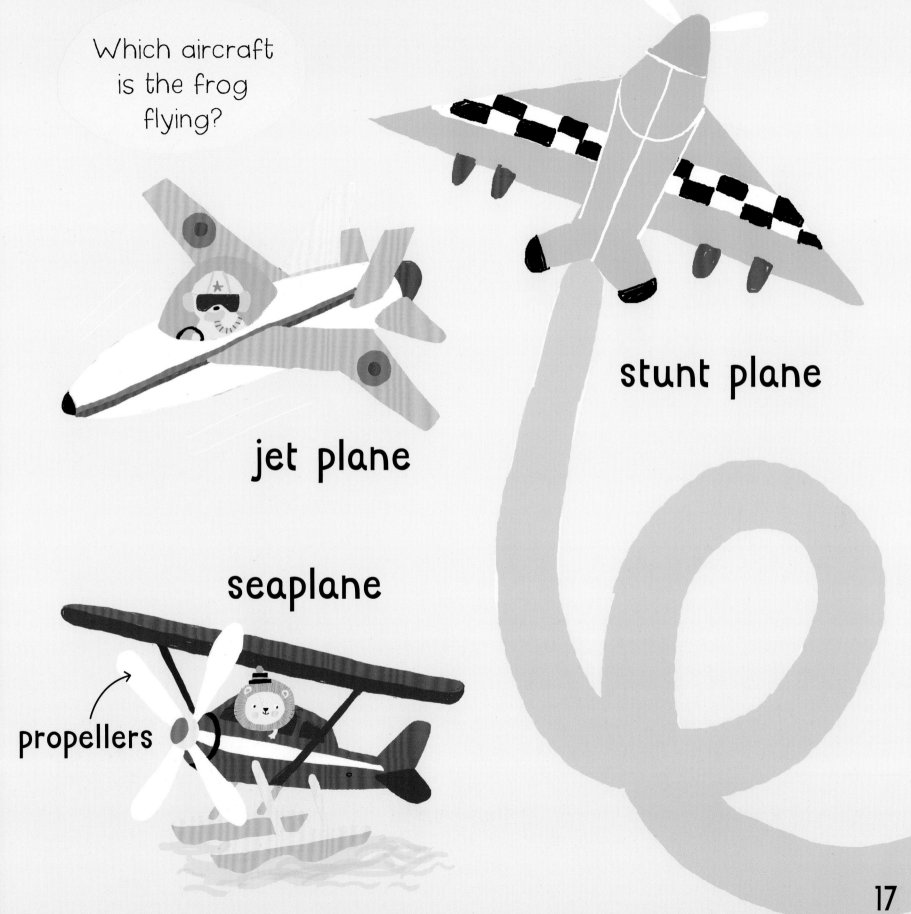

Which aircraft is the frog flying?

stunt plane

jet plane

seaplane

propellers

# Tough trucks

Big and strong! Trucks can push and pull, and do lots of different jobs.

road sweeping truck

sweeping brush

Whose car has broken down?

tow truck

recycling
truck

What
items can be
recycled?

flatbed truck

snow plough

Trucks transport all sorts of cargo, from cars to milk.

delivery van

How many cars are being transported?

car transporter

lorry

What food
and drink can
you spot?

tank truck

Milk

road train

21

# Fun time

It would be fun to ride on one of these! Which is your favourite?

Segway

How many hats can you find?

Who is riding the cable car?

monster truck

go kart

cable car

snowmobile

golf cart

sledge

Some vehicles go on holiday!
Which one of these would you
most like to spend a week in?

Which vehicles
are facing left and
which right?

How many
flowers can
you see?

campervan

24

caravan and car

Which vehicle
do you think is
the biggest?

recreational vehicle

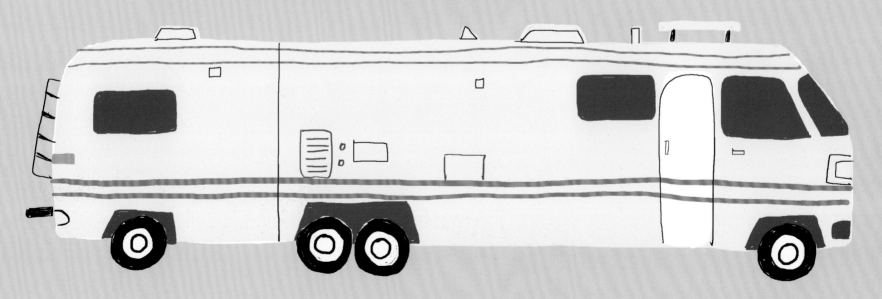

# All aboard!

Boats and ships travel on water, carrying passengers or goods.

Can you find the crab?

fishing boat

anchor

fishing net

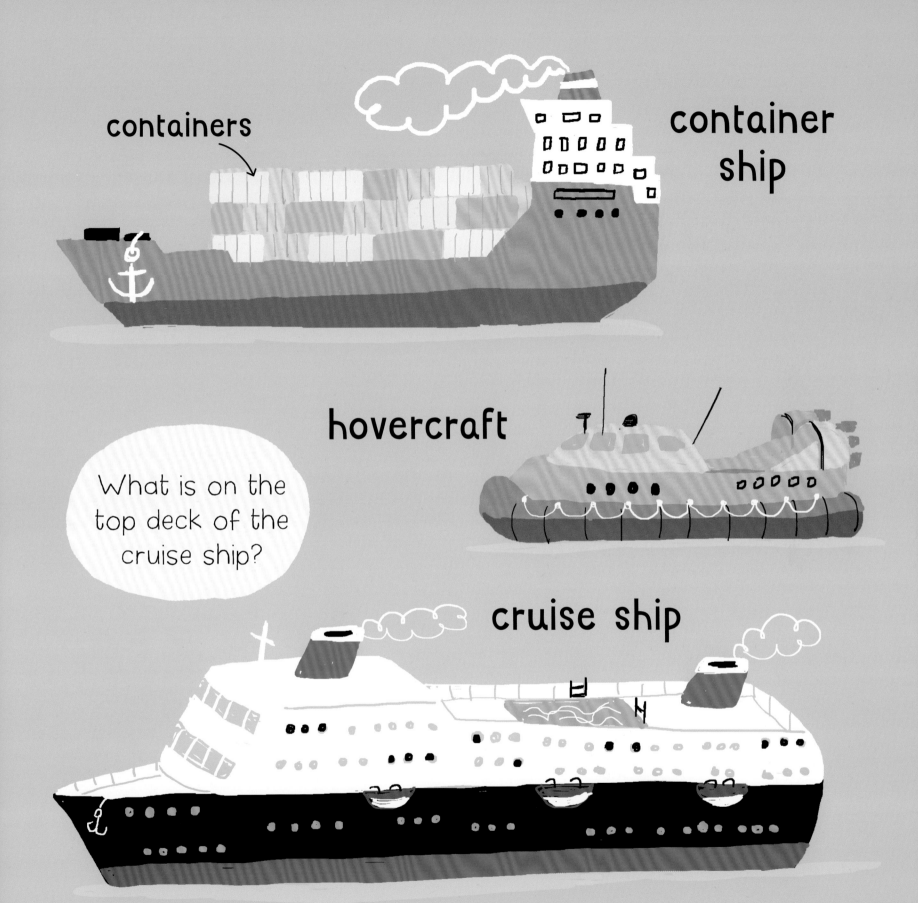

containers

container
ship

hovercraft

What is on the
top deck of the
cruise ship?

cruise ship

Not all water transport is big. Some can move along with just one person sailing or paddling.

**speedboat**

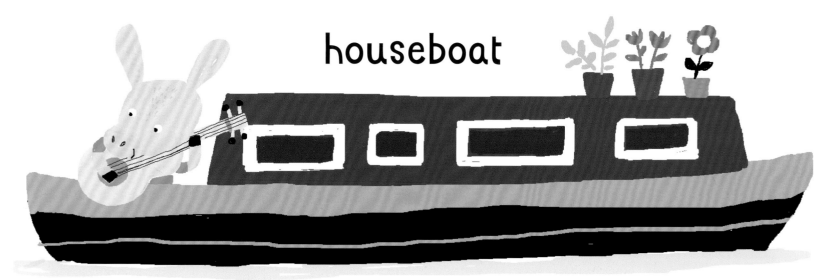

**houseboat**

**yacht**

sail

oar

**rowing boat**

jet ski

kayak

paddle

Which vehicle travels underwater?

submarine

catamaran

# On tracks

Trains and trams move by running along tracks.

How many crates is the freight train pulling?

## steam train

## freight train

5 x 30

# bullet train

Which train is the tiger driving?

# passenger train

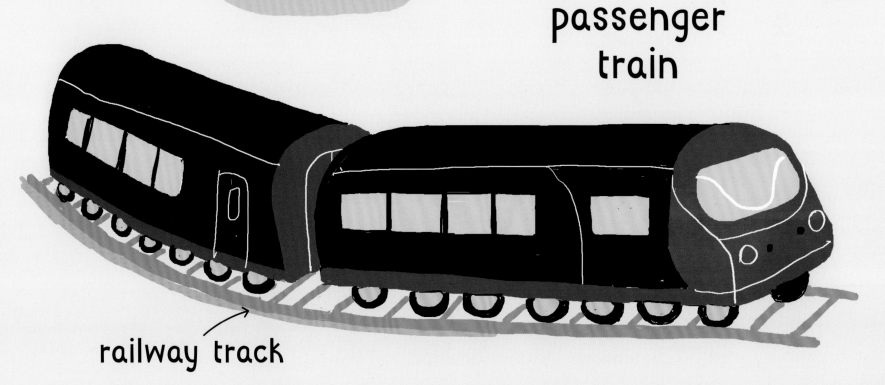

railway track

Some trains are super speedy, while others travel through public streets.

tunnel

underground train

funicular train

Which train clears snow from tracks?

tram

snow plough train

double decker train

maglev

On which train can you sit upstairs?

33

# Working hard

Powerful machines are used to move earth and help to build houses and roads.

How many hard hats can you spot?

dumper truck

digger

caterpillar tracks

bucket

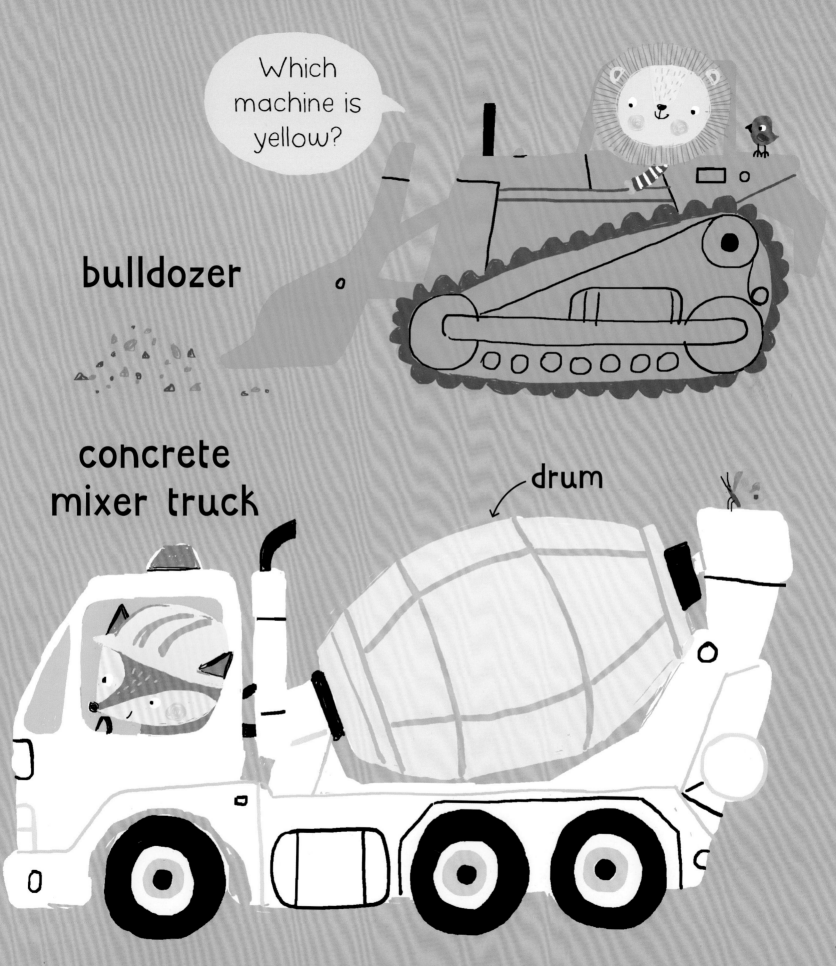

35

Strong machines can help with
all sorts of jobs.

Can you
find two orange
traffic cones?

forklift truck

road roller

paver

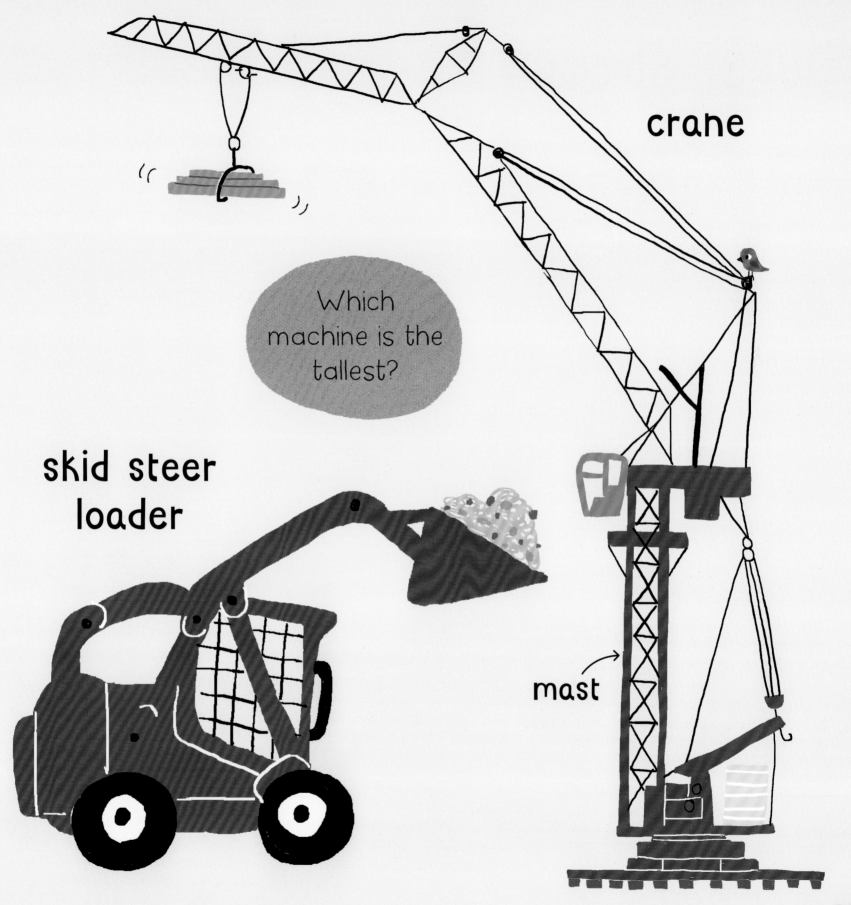

crane

Which machine is the tallest?

skid steer loader

mast

# Super speedy

Some vehicles race and they have to be fast to be first across the finish line. 3-2-1-Go!

drag car

Which three numbers can you see?

What colour is the rally car?

Formula One car

superbike

rally car

43

supersonic
car

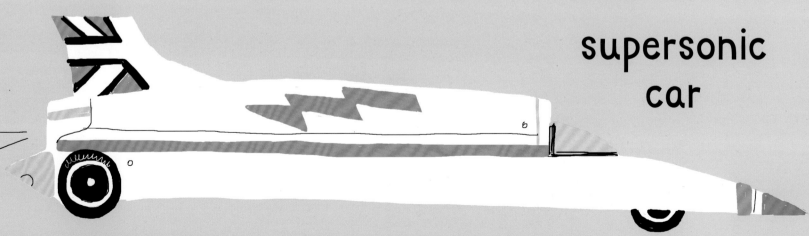

Which vehicle would you most like to race in? Would you drive on your own, or as part of a team with your friends?

Which vehicle can fly?

aerobatic plane

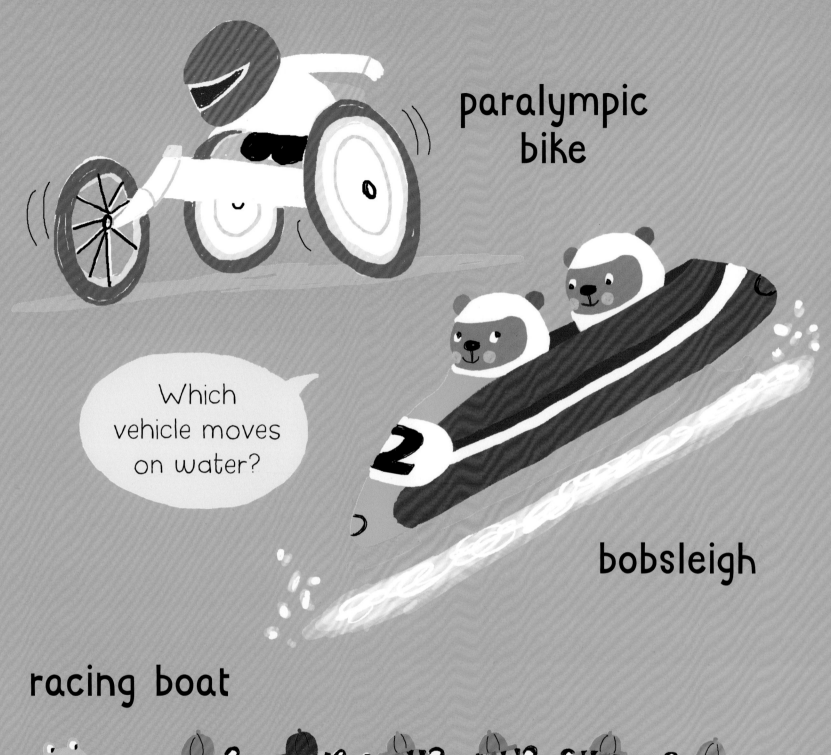

paralympic bike

bobsleigh

Which vehicle moves on water?

racing boat

41

# Farm fun

Tractors are used on farms. They can pull heavy machines that help farmers do their work.

bucket

How many birds can you spot?

wide tractor

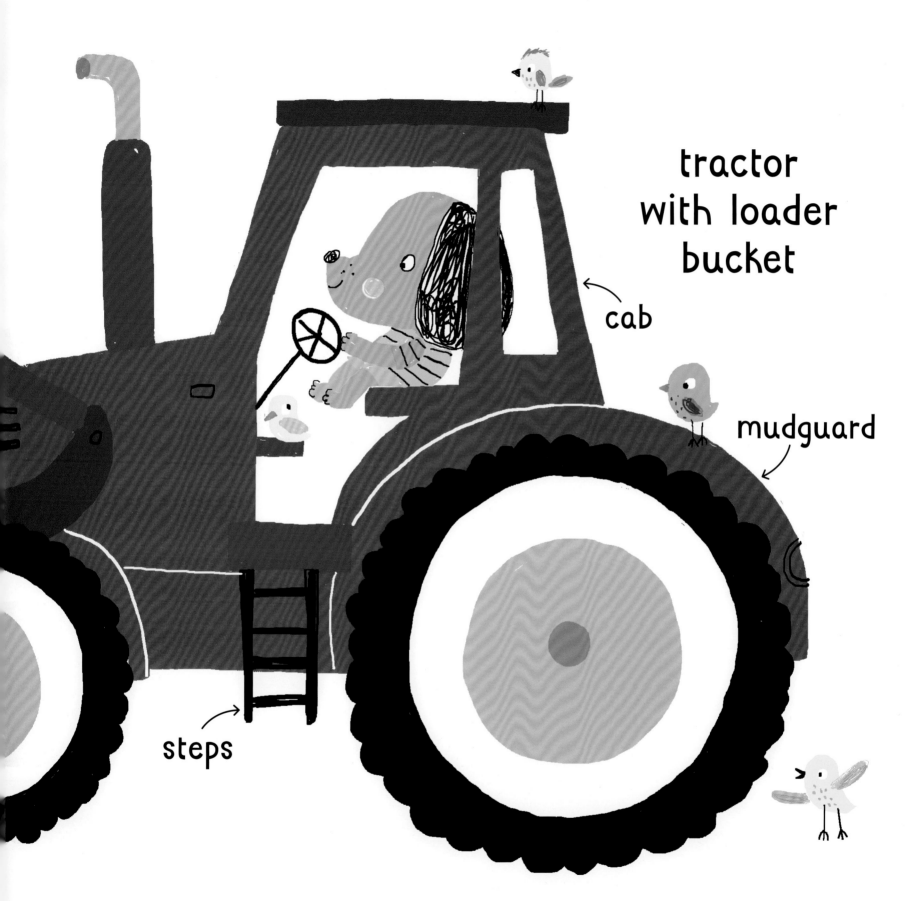

tractor
with loader
bucket

cab

mudguard

steps

Farmers use machines to help them transport animals and gather crops.

**truck with trailer**

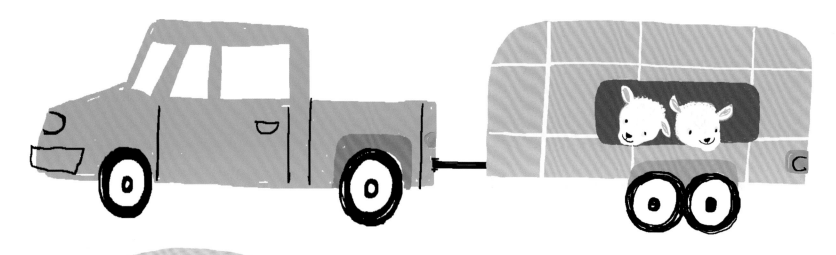

What is the combine harvester cutting?

**tractor with plough**

44

tractor with baler

Which vehicle is collecting bales of hay?

combine harvester

# Numbers

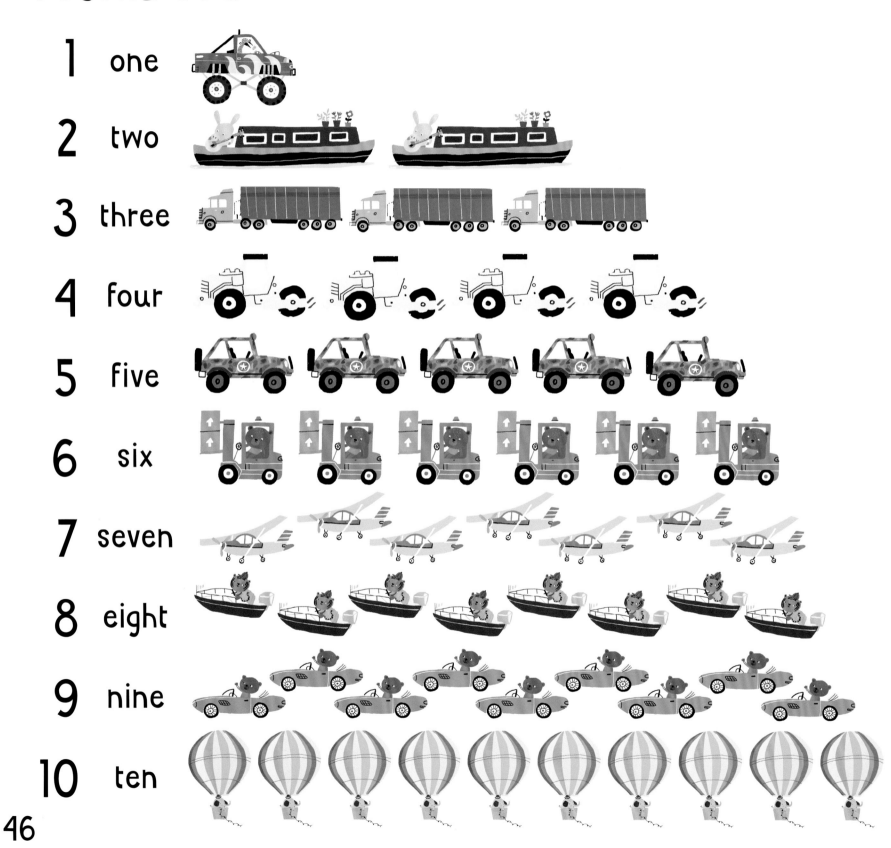

1 one

2 two

3 three

4 four

5 five

6 six

7 seven

8 eight

9 nine

10 ten

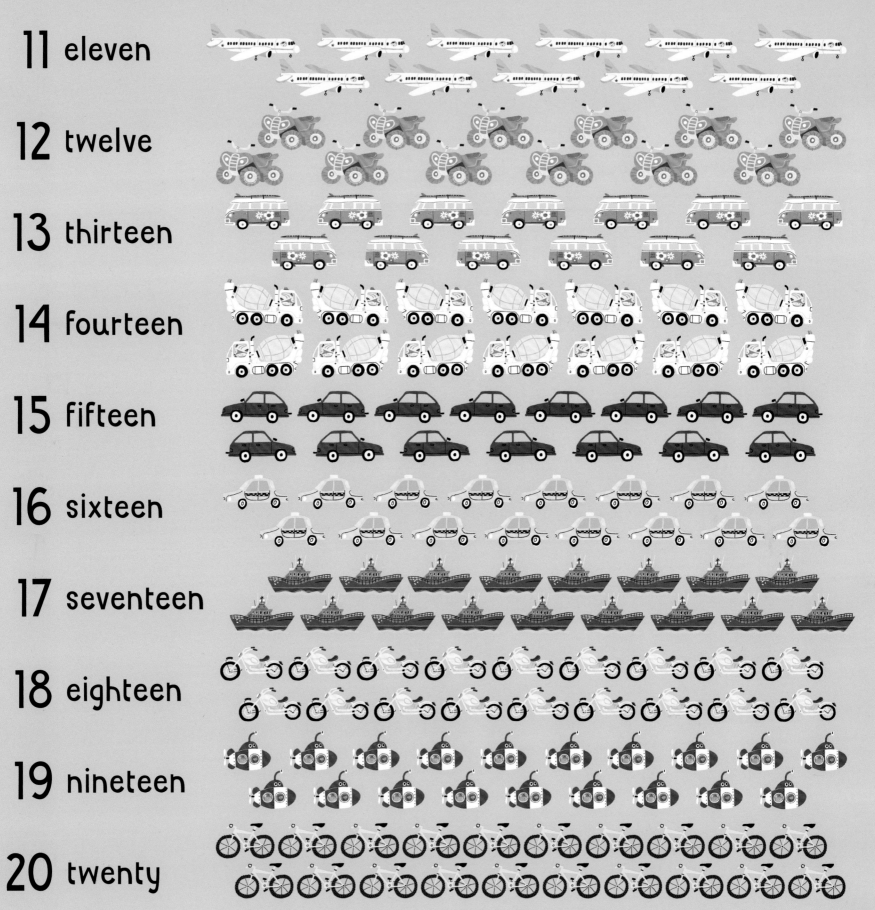

11 eleven

12 twelve

13 thirteen

14 fourteen

15 fifteen

16 sixteen

17 seventeen

18 eighteen

19 nineteen

20 twenty

# Colours

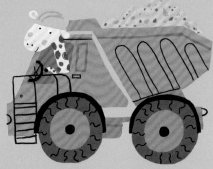

**orange** dumper truck

**blue** speedboat

**red** fire engine

**white** ambulance

**yellow** digger

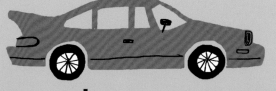

**grey** van

**pink** bus

**green** recycling truck

**purple** sports car

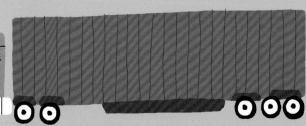

**black** train

**brown** lorry